Wet

Water

A New Approach to Thriving in the
Workplace

Lon Schiffbauer, Ph.D.

A Thriving Workplace
Salt Lake City, Utah

Wet Water

A New Approach to Thriving in the Workplace

Published by

A Thriving Workplace

Salt Lake City, Utah

ISBN-13: 978-0615921679 (A Thriving Workplace)

ISBN-10: 0615921671

www.AThrivingWorkplace.com

Chapter 1

Wet Water?

We've all felt it. Frustration at work, dissatisfaction with our jobs, dysfunctional relationships with coworkers, absence of trust in our leaders, lack of recognition and appreciation for our contributions. It all seems to be part and parcel with what it means to be an employee in today's workplace. Of course there are also moments of triumph and exhilaration, times when we feel a real sense of worth and accomplishment in what we do. But these seem to be little more than flashes in the pan in an otherwise never-ending struggle to eke out a living and, hopefully, find some semblance of personal self-worth in the process.

The good news is that it's possible to tip the scales, and we don't have to quit our jobs to do it. We can increase our sense of meaning and purpose while at the same time reduce our feelings of futility and frustration. But to do this we first need to understand what it is that's causing us such discontent. And to do this, we need to talk about wet water.

Water is wet. (Really. Go check. I'll wait.) That's its nature, and for the most part that's not a problem. Fish do quite well in wet water. A fish doesn't complain that water is wet. If it did it would live a very frustrated and pointless existence. Even if it wanted to, even if it dedicated its every waking moment to the endeavor, a fish can't change the nature of wet water. It's an environmental constant. All a fish can hope to do is adapt to water's wet nature and live in harmony with its environment.

Like fish, we live in many environmental constants that cannot be changed, but unlike fish, we sometimes get it into our heads that these constants have to change for us to be happy. So we embark on a frustrating and ultimately futile journey as we try to change our environmental constants. In other words, we try to make water not wet.

When this happens something does have to change, and it's not the water.

Chapter 2

Wet Water and Environmental Constants

Unlike fish, we don't live it wet water. However, we do live in a universe of environmental constants. Fighting these environmental constants makes about as much sense as a fish attempting to change the nature of wet water. And yet oh how we try! What might an environmental constant look like for us? Well, let me introduce you to Sisyphus.

As far as scoundrels went, Sisyphus was a real piece of work. Abundantly cleaver and deceitful, the Greek antihero used his considerable gifts to torment those around him. One moment he would welcome travelers into his home as his guests; the next he would murder them and toss their bodies out into the streets to be devoured by wild beasts. Crafty and avaricious, he seduced his niece and stole his brother's throne. An equal opportunity tormentor, he brought no end of grief to the gods of Olympus as well. One day, on a lark, he decided to spread stories of Zeus' sexual exploits all over town. Well as it turns out the king of the gods was not amused by this little prank, so Zeus commanded Hades to personally go up with a pair of handcuffs and collect Sisyphus himself. But our friend still had a few tricks up his tunic. Feigning interest in the curious handcuffs, the wily Sisyphus asked Hades to demonstrate how the things worked, which the god of the underworld did—on himself. Before he knew it Hades was locked in a closet while all around world the cycle of life and death went all catawampus. Yep, Sisyphus was a character, alright.

Eventually though things caught up with Sisyphus. He was finally dragged down to the underworld where the gods had devised a beautifully ingenious fate, worthy of Sisyphus' wit. As punishment, Sisyphus was damned to an eternity of rolling a bolder up a giant hill, only to have the immense stone slip away just inches from the top and roll back to the valley below. Over and over, without end, Sisyphus would follow the bolder down to the bottom, set his shoulder against the great rock, and start the process all over again.

It's scarcely possible to think of a more diabolical fate. A task so repetitive and endless, so taxing, so completely and utterly meaningless, one wonders how anything could be worse.

Then again, that might sound like where we work.

It may feel like there are times when Sisyphus' fate is not completely dissimilar from our own. Work can often seem mind-numbingly tedious, repetitive, and pointless. Recognition for our efforts can be infrequent, haphazard, and unequal to the value we bring to the company. (Anyone that has ever received a $25 gift card to Wal-Mart for working nights and weekends on a project for three months knows what I mean.) Sometimes it can be hard to see how our labors amount to anything, especially in a large corporate setting. The harder, faster, or smarter we work, the more our responsibilities pile up. Those that stick around long enough see history repeat itself as one business fad replaces another. Ideas and strategies are tried, forgotten, then thought of again by someone else and the cycle starts all over again. And at the end of the day, do our accomplishments really amount to anything? In most cases the company could continue on just fine with or without us, so what's the point of it all?

Sisyphus' environmental constant was his punishment to roll the stone to the top of the hill. Nothing could change this. The gods had decreed it, and there's no use in fighting the gods. The nature of the workplace is often very similar. To fight it or insist that it be changed is an exercise in futility.

So is that it? Is Sisyphus doomed to be eternally miserable in these unchanging environmental constants? Not necessarily. And neither are we. But to learn how to find a sense of purpose in the face of pointlessness, we first need to understand what is it about these environmental constants that makes us so miserable.

Chapter 3

Environmental Constants and False Conditions

When we insist that an environmental constant has to change before we can feel a sense of satisfaction, purpose, and meaning in our jobs, we're insisting on conditions that are unattainable, or as I call them, false conditions.

A false condition is an environmental state that we perceive as necessary for our happiness but which does not or cannot exist. In other words, it's something we tell ourselves we need to be happy, but that we can never have. For the fish, his false condition would be insisting that he can only be happy once the water is not so wet. For Sisyphus, his false condition was believing that he needed to roll the stone to the top of the hill before he could feel a sense of accomplishment and purpose. Water will always be wet and the stone will always roll back down, so insisting that things be otherwise is pointless.

We, too, have false conditions that we erect to keep ourselves miserable. If we want to find a sense of fulfillment, meaning, and purpose at work, the first thing we need to do is learn to recognize our false conditions.

Broadly speaking, there are four kinds of false conditions. We'll go over these in more detail shortly, but let's take just a peek.

The first is insisting that environmental constants must change before we can feel a sense of purpose and fulfillment. For example, insisting that you'll never be happy until people all over the world treat each other with nothing but sincere kindness and love is not very realistic. Yes, it would be wonderful, but not likely to happen any time soon.

The second is by attaching a moral value to something which intrinsically has none. The world of fashion is a bastion of this kind of thinking. Last year's jacket, something that was once considered cool and chic, is now looked upon as outdated and heinous, when at the end of the day it's neither good or bad. It's just a bunch of fabric.

The third is allowing societal measures to distort our view of our worth as a person. Unless we're careful, easy-to-quantify things such as salary, position, or physical appearance can cause us to measure our own worth by others' yardsticks rather than our own.

The fourth is allowing the feelings of expectation and entitlement to tell us what we think we should have. Thinking that you should have more can make what you have now seem inadequate, yet it's more than what you had when you came into this world, and more than you'll have when you leave it.

So that's a taste. Now let's explore some of these false conditions in greater detail and see how they prevent us from thriving at work.

Chapter 4

False Condition #1: It's Time for Change!

Politicians are always fond of promising change. As voters we clamor for things to be done differently so politicians are only too happy to promise that, if elected, it won't be business as usual. And so we elect them, then wait for all the wonderful change we'd been promised to fall on us like rain. But it never does. It's the same old same old. When that happens we become frustrated and so two years later send out the rallying call once again, this time calling for *real* change (as though apparently we weren't clear about what change was the last time around). And the cycle repeats itself.

It seems like our desire for change is constant. We want better pay, more benefits, greater respect at work, better career opportunities, more time with our families, a shorter commute, a bigger office, and so on. We seem hard-wired to identify those things that we consider lacking and insist that they be rectified. The problem is that many of the problems we find are environmental constants and yet we insist that they are preventing us from feeling fulfillment at work.

Let me give you an example.

One day my son started a new job. He was just out of high school and wasn't quite ready to head off to college yet, so his vocational options were few. He ended up taking a job with a fast food joint in the local mall. After his first week he told me that he didn't like his new job very much, mostly because his boss was from Thailand and had a thick accent that was difficult to understand. He told me how much better it would be if she could just speak English. I agreed, but pointed out that the chances of this person developing fluent English devoid of any accent over the next few months for his benefit was not very likely, so it might be better that he drop this as a requirement for enjoying his new position.

Sure, we might have more education and experience in the workplace than my son, but we do the same thing. We think about how much better it would be if our managers practiced better decision-making, if we had more time to complete a project, if our co-workers were better team players, if our bonuses better reflected our individual accomplishments, if there wasn't such favoritism in the workplace, and so on. Granted, these can all be very frustrating and at times make us want to scream, but in most cases they are environmental constants and not likely to change any time soon. Making our happiness contingent on these sort of things is a classic false condition.

Chapter 5

False Condition #2: Bad Weather

When I was young and first learning French I was completely perplexed by the notion that objects had genders. A fork is feminine, but a knife is masculine. A car is feminine; a bicycle is masculine. Cup, feminine; glass, masculine. Everything had a gender. It drove me nuts! I complained constantly that this was ridiculous and that French would be so much easier to learn if it were to drop this nonsensical anachronism. (Talk a false condition! I'm sure the French people would be only too happy to change their language for my benefit.)

We do the same thing—not with genders but with value judgments. We have a tendency to assign moral values to things that are amoral. Shakespeare's Hamlet once said, "There is nothing either good or bad, but thinking makes it so". How right he was. We often talk in terms "good" weather or "bad" weather when really there's no such thing as either. There's only weather. Our perception of the weather is dependent on what we want to do in it. Windy weather is great for sailing but awful for cycling.

The problem with attaching a value to an environmental constant is that it feeds our desire to change or fight that which we perceive as wrong. Imagine how much more miserable the fish would be if he decided that not only was wet water undesirable but that it was morally wrong as well!

What does this look like in the workplace? How about the size or color of our cubicles or offices, the amount of time we have to wait to get an elevator, or the selection of sodas in the break room? At what point does the size of a cubical become good? Eight feet? Twelve? Twenty? And how about gray versus green? Is one more virtuous than the other? Is a one-minute wait morally superior to three? Coke more virtuous than Pepsi? (My wife would say yes.) I'm not saying that some conditions are not more preferable than others, but saying that it's "wrong" that you should have to wait three minutes for an elevator is a false condition. There's nothing "wrong" with three minutes, and insisting that there is does not make it so. The value of those three minutes is decided by what we do with them.

Chapter 6

False Condition #3: I'm Entitled to It

Consider this scenario: You go out to your car one morning, turn the key, and the engine starts. What do you feel? Probably not a whole lot. It's what you expected to have happen when you turned the key. It's not like the thing just turned water into wine or anything. Besides, purchasing the car entitles you to a vehicle that performs as the manufacturer promised.

Now see yourself going out to your car one cold morning, turning the key, and hearing a roar, a sputter, followed by a loud *bang*, then finally silence. Now what do you feel? Annoyance? Frustration? Dread at the thought of how much this is going to cost you?

Whatever your feelings, chances are they are rooted in your sense of expectation and entitlement. Perhaps no other perceptions are as poisonous to our sense of fulfillment than entitlement and expectation. They are the feelings that tell us that we're not happy, that we should have more, that we deserve better. Remember the cube we talked about earlier? The perceptions of expectation and entitlement are what tell us that we should have a bigger cube, a nicer car, or a bigger bonus. They magnify the gap between what we have and what we feel we should have, whereas gratitude focuses our attention on what we have and how rich we truly are. When expectation and entitlement rule the day we become dissatisfied with our current circumstance. That's when we start giving power to our false conditions.

Chapter 7

False Condition #4: Keeping Up with the Jones'

A close friend of mine and her husband once decided that they wanted to take a different track in their lives. Both were well-paid managers for a large global corporation, but both felt unfulfilled. He wanted to be a high school teacher, while she wanted to start her own consulting business. Problem was, their mortgage took the income of two corporate managers. There was no way that a high school teacher and a fledgling home businesswoman could pay for their gorgeous 6,000-square-foot McMansion. Furthermore, the idea of selling their home, downsizing, and paying cash outright for smaller home was very attractive. Who wouldn't want to live without a mortgage, right? So that's what they did. They sold their home, got a wonderful price, then turned around and bought a nice little 3,000-square-foot fixer-upper for cash.

Pretty sweet, eh?

My friend spent two weeks crying in her bedroom.

Later, after she had used up her supply of tissues and had some time to think about it, she realized that she had based a great deal of her self-worth on the external trappings of success. A large beautiful home told the world—and consequently herself—that she was a valuable person with purpose. However, as with most of us, she didn't realize that she felt this way until after the material vestiges of her success had been taken away.

We all want to live a meaningful life, one that can be considered valuable. The problem is that quantifying a meaningful life can be very difficult. It requires a great deal of introspection and soul searching, working to identify those things that are truly important to us. This can be hard, not to mention painful. After all, who wants to go through this process and discover that they're a waste of space? Luckily, society has developed all sorts of ingenious methods for quantifying one's worth as a human being. Things like salary, level of education, the speed of our cars, or in the case of my friend, the size of our homes. Think about it. What better way to sum up one's worth than with nice clear numbers like $100,000 a year, 6 years of post-graduate education, 0 to 60 in 5.4 seconds, or 6,000 square feet? What's more, it's a universal measurement. Everyone in the country is on the same scale so with little more than a quick glance we can determine just how re rank against everyone else.

Granted, letting go of such easy-to-understand measurements is very difficult, especially when they are supported by processes that lend an air of legitimacy to the measurement. Consider for a moment a performance review. Many corporations have extremely thorough and exhaustive review processes, supported by statistical and individual data. This gives the process—and consequently the review at the end of the process—a sense of authority and credibility. As a result it can be very difficult to stand up against a poor performance review and not allow it to become a verdict of your entire existence. After all, the numbers don't lie, right?

It's important that we don't abdicate the responsibility of evaluating our self-worth to someone else. Like the gods who sought to punish Sisyphus, many will try to dictate the terms whereby we evaluate our own worth. Sure, deciding what it means to live a meaningful life can be a difficult process. It involves deciding what's most important to us and what behaviors need to support that belief. We may say that something is important to us, but when we look at what our actions really say the truth may be hard to face. But face it we must. Either that or continue to let others determine how we should feel about ourselves.

Chapter 8

Your Own Private Idaho

Not everyone clings to the same false conditions. We all bang our heads against different unchanging environmental realities. Remember that we create false conditions for ourselves when we fight environmental constants. These environmental constants are often decided by the company we work for, its corporate culture, the career path we've chosen, the industry, or how we think the world should be. However, some environmental constants seem to permeate all others, and in my opinion, the most universal of these is human behavior. Simply put, nothing can be remotely as mind-boggling as how we behave and interact with one another, especially at work. To be sure, the workplace can be a confusing and frustrating environment. From comic strips like *Dilbert*, television programs such as *The Office*, and movies like *Office Space*, we enjoy exploring the absurdity of the workplace. Entire libraries could be filled with work stories that make us gasp in terror one moment and shoot milk through our noses the next.

Don't believe me? Watch.

Chapter 9

Why Are People So Messed Up?

Reality TV. We just can't seem to get enough of it. *Cops, 16 & Pregnant, The Amazing Race, The Apprentice, Survivor, The Bachelor, Big Brother, The Celebrity Rehab, MTV's Real World,* the list seems endless. All over the world viewers are making reality TV shows the top rated programs.

There are many reasons why these shows are so popular. For starters, they're wildly unpredictable and exciting to watch. As welcomed voyeurs in the lives of some amazingly colorful people, we find ourselves rooting for our heroes and groaning with disbelief when the bad guys come out on top. And because we think the people and situations in these shows are real (as opposed actors following a script), we attach a greater level of importance on the outcome. Reality TV shows also have an ability to prick our moral and ethical sensibilities more so than fictional drama. Because aspects of these programs are purportedly real, we feel empathy and compassion when we see an animal suffering or someone struggling with a disability. But there's another, perhaps more sinister side to this coin. Some elements of these reality shows appeal to our baser instincts, conjuring up those same feelings that spectators perhaps felt as they witnesses gladiators maul each other in the colosseums. We watch dumbfounded as people engage in some of the most outrageous and unthinkable behavior imaginable. Unapologetic backstabbing, name-calling, verbal abuse, lies stacked on lies, and rationalization of the most shallow sort, all abundantly provided for our viewing pleasure. Why we seem to love this so much is hard to say. Maybe seeing the problems of others makes our own seem relatively small by comparison. Or maybe we enjoy a sense of vindication that tells us that while we've done some pretty stupid things in our lives, at least we're not that bad! None of us like to think we're idiots, so watching someone else behave far worse than we think we ever would can help us feel better about ourselves.

Whatever the reason, one thing that's safe to say, we're fascinated by human behavior.

We find outrageous and absurd behavior captivating in part because we like to consider ourselves rational beings, so when someone freaks out on screen we seem drawn like moths to a flame. But are we really so rational? Let's take a moment and look at some of the things that make up human behavior.

Chapter 10

Blame it on Darwin

Ever had your appendix removed? Chances are you or someone you know has. So what is that thing anyway? What does it do? Well, as it turns out, not much. All it seems to be good for these days is getting infected and putting us in the hospital. Oh sure, it probably served some purpose early on in human evolution, but today it's about as useful as a whale's hind legs. (Yep, they still have them.)

Like our physical selves, there are behavioral remnants of evolution that serve little purpose today but can really make a mess of things. Take the principle of fight-or-flight, for example. We encounter a dangerous situation and our bodies respond. Our pupils dilate, our hearts beat faster, breathing increases as our airways open in anticipation. Nonessential blood vessels constrict while those of organs that might be called upon to respond, such as skeletal and cardiac muscles, dilate to increase blood flow. The digestive system shuts down while blood glucose levels rise and the adrenal glands furiously pump adrenaline into the system. Now we're ready to rumble (or run like a dickens)! Problem is we're not running from a ravenous bear or protecting our herd from marauders. We're sitting in a meeting, hearing someone sabotage our project right there before our eyes, in front of our peers, supervisors, and customers. And as satisfying as it may be to walk over and slug the guy then bolt for the door, this isn't really an option. The physiological responses we need to be successful today have changed since the days we had to fight with mountain lions to get our next meal, but somewhere along the way evolution didn't get the memo. Think of it as a brand-new computer complete with old software preinstalled that you will never use but still manages to muck up the operating system now and again. We come preinstalled with many features that only seem to be good for getting us into trouble.

Chapter 11

It's in Your Genes

I once heard my father telling a friend of his about how he raised my brother and me. We were just two years apart and had pretty much the same childhoods. We had identical rooms, ate the same food, wore the same cloths, and attended the same schools. Then my father told his friend, "One became a drug dealer, the other became a Christian missionary." (I'll let the reader decide which one I might have been.)

Each one of us is a completely unique person. Even identical twins have different fingerprints. This is the result of countless genetic mutations that have occurred in our families' histories. Think back to Biology 101. Our DNA and genome contain the blueprints that make us who we are, and as they go about doing their jobs, mutations take place. These genetic mutations can occur during cell division or by exposure to mutagens such as radiation, mutagenic chemicals, or certain types of viruses. Mutations can even be induced by the organism itself through standard cellular processes or introduced from one or both of the parents' reproductive cells. As the genes come together to form the chromosomes these mutations can manifest themselves as micro-deletions, duplications, translocations, or inversions. Mutations are a regular part of the cellular process and help to contribute to a healthy and vibrant gene pool.

The vast majority of mutations have no measurable effect on the fitness of the organism, but some can have profound effects. Take my son Brandon, for example. He has a neuro-genetic disorder known Angelman Syndrome. It's caused by a micro-deletion of a tiny portion of the 15th chromosome on his mother's side. The mutation affects a minuscule piece of a chromosome in a microscopic DNA strain, but the results are profound. The condition is characterized by general developmental delay, lack of speech, walking and balance disorders, hypermotoric behavior, tongue-thrusting, spontaneous laughter, seizures, jerky movements, ataxia, and sleep disorders. In fact, my son's psychomotor and mental development is so severely delayed that he will never develop the motor skills past that of a one-year old child, even though he's a fully-grown adult.

All of this begs the question: If such an indescribably small mutation in a person's chromosome—one that a few decades ago could not have been observed at the genetic level—can have such a sweeping effect on a person's development and behavior, what other behavioral characteristics might be the result of seemingly neutral or imperceptible genetic variations that occur in each one of us?

Chapter 12

It's Something in the Water

The flip-side of this equation is nurture—the effects that our environment can have on who we are. From the time we came into this world it has been helping to forge our opinions, attitudes, beliefs, perceptions, and behaviors. The culture in which we're born—our religious background, our economic status, our family and friends, the education afforded us, the social/political systems of the country in which we live—all help to mold us into the people we are today.

Throughout history many philosophers have compared a newborn babe to a blank slate, ready for a lifetime of experiences to create a personality. Of course we now know that evolution and genetics play their part in driving our behavior, but there can be little doubt that our physical environments have a great deal to do with what sort of people we become.

In its most basic form the effect of nurture is easy to see. Behavior that is considered positive and beneficial is rewarded and therefore reinforced, while less-desirable behavior is frowned upon and punished. This makes sense, until we consider what happens when the rules of the game change and the need for the behavior changes.

Take the case of five monkeys. One day a group of researchers placed five monkeys in a room. Inside this room was a mechanism that, when actuated, provided a reward in the form of a treat that all the monkeys just loved. (They went ape over it! Get it? Ape? Anyway...) However, whenever one of the monkeys would go near the mechanism the researchers would spray the other four monkeys with cold water. This was the environmental input —the "nurture". Well the other monkeys didn't like this one bit, so every time a monkey would even look at that darned mechanism the others would pounce on him and beat him up. The message was clear: No tasty treats or you'll get a whooping. So after a while the monkeys stopped trying to get treats. Then the researchers did something interesting. They substituted one of the monkeys for a new one. This new monkey recognized the mechanism but had never been sprayed with cold water and so went right for the treats. The other four monkeys, afraid of the cold shower that was sure to come, did what you might have expected. They ganged up on the new monkey and beat him up. Before long the new monkey as well stopped trying to get a treat. Then the researchers substituted a second monkey, and the same thing happened. The second monkey went for the treats and the others clobbered him, except this time the first monkey that had been substituted joined in on the beating. This went on until all five monkeys had been switched out. All that remained were five monkeys that had never been sprayed with cold water and yet would beat up any monkey that tried to go for the treats. If we could ask these guys why they did this, chances are they'd say something like, "That's just how things are done around here."

Chapter 13

Maslow Was Right

Have you ever noticed how incredibly immature otherwise sensible and rational adults can be sometimes? Think of the way that a black light can illuminate bright and vibrant florescent colors that otherwise would be invisible to the naked eye. As children, our need for love, affirmation, belonging, and security are natural and raw. Age and experience—what we call maturity—paints layers over these stark florescent colors to where they become all but gone. But they are not gone. They're still there, lying underneath the surface, invisible to even ourselves. But once in a while circumstance pulls out a black light and shines it on us. Maybe it's in a harsh performance review that we were not expecting, or maybe when we're pulled into an office and told that we're being downsized. These experiences have the ability to shine a black light on our most basic needs for security and belonging.

Maslow's Hierarchy of Needs tells us that everything we need to be healthy and happy is reliant on our most basic needs for such things as food, security, the availability of resources, health, and family. Without first meeting these needs we cannot go on to reach for the more noble goals of life, such as self-esteem, confidence, creativity, and spontaneity. In many ways our ability to meet these basic needs is directly tied to our jobs. (More about that later.) For most of us our employment is what allows us to buy food, pay the mortgage, access healthcare, and provide for our families. All of this means that when we perceive our employment as being in jeopardy we might perceive everything we are as somehow being under threat. This can bring our scared inner-child screaming to the surface!

Our childhood fears and insecurities have not left; their needs have simply become more sophisticated. Where a child worries about being loved by its mother, we worry about being appreciated by our bosses. Where a child worries about having a nurturing home, we worry about having a secure position. When a child feels that its love or place in the home is at risk, its fears and insecurities manifest themselves in way of moping or tantrums. Likewise, even as adults our fears and insecurities can exhibit themselves in strikingly similar ways.

Chapter 14

It's Getting Crowded in Here

No one lives outside of a group. Even a hermit defines his existence in part through the group. After all, without the group he would have nothing to run from. Living as part of a group affects our behavior just as does evolution, nature, and nurture. As we saw from our monkey example, groups require us to take on roles as we come to understand the group's expectations of our behavior. These roles in turn can determine how we interact with one another and the nature of these interactions. We assume norms determined by the group, rules of conduct for group members. What to wear, how to speak, what's considered good manners. All of these are examples of norms that we assume to be an accepted and contributing group member. This helps develop cohesion, a sense of pride, trust, and commitment to the group and its members.

But there are the side-effects of group behaviors that run the risk of luring members away from the best course of action. For example, groupthink can drive people to a bad course of action, all in the interest of seeking concurrence among group members. In these cases the value of agreement among group members is placed above that of finding the right answer. Also, we've all seen or experienced instances in which ideas were squelched or withheld because they ran the risk of disagreeing with a group leader or the direction the group seemed to be heading. These and other less-than-helpful practices are very common phenomena in many work groups.

Another thing to consider is the interactions between groups themselves. Perhaps nothing can better demonstrate the paradoxical nature of this type of group psychology than religion. For the most part all religions espouse positive, wholesome principles like love, compassion, charity, and mercy. And yet, when put together on the world stage, many of these groups find themselves at odds with one another, sometimes even coming to blows. Some people try to cite this as evidence that religion is a bad thing, but really these religious groups are behaving as do all groups, whether they be religions, political parties, nationalities, ethnicities, genders, or any other category we humans can contrive. All one needs to do is listen to the vitriolic rhetoric of the political parties to see what I mean. Both are equally committed to the good of the country and its people, yet to listen to them you'd think that the other is spawned from pond scum.

The groups that make up the workplace are no less susceptible to these and other group dynamics.

Chapter 15

See the Strings

But wait. Hold it. You and I are human beings, too. Right? Does that mean that we're as much the result of evolution, genetics, upbringing, psychology, and group dynamics as all these morons we work with?

Yep.

But knowing is half the battle. (*G.I. Jooooe!*)

Ever read comic books? You should. Good stuff out there. In the comic book series *Watchmen* there's a character called Dr. Manhattan, a superhero created when Jon Osterman was accidently trapped in an Intrinsic Filed Subtractor. (You see, *that's* why your mother told you not to play in that thing.) As his name might suggest, Dr. Manhattan's powers were based on quantum physics and atomic principles. He had the power of teleportation, death rays, flight. You know, the usual. There was also something that he could do that used to drive all of those around him absolutely bonkers: He could see time as one eternal now. Everything that had ever been, was now, and would ever be he could see as though it were happening right in front of him at that very moment. And if that wasn't weird enough, he could see his own future too, but apart from his present. I'll show you what I mean.

In one scene in the ninth book Dr. Manhattan is talking with Laurie, his old girlfriend. At one point he tells her that this is where they would hold their conversation, and that it would start when she would surprise him by telling him that she's seeing another man.

"You know about Dan?" she asks.

"No. Not yet," he says. "But in a few moments you're going to tell me."

Huh?

Later, in the course of the conversation the news does come out, and Dr. Manhattan is indeed surprised.

This drives Laurie nuts!

"Why does my perception of time disturb you?" Dr. Manhattan asks.

"Why ask?" She says. "You already know my answer: It's stupid!" She then asks why he was surprised that something would happen even when he knew it would.

"Everything is preordained. Even my responses," he tells her.

"And you just go through the motions, acting them out?" Laurie asks. "Is that what you are? The most powerful thing in the universe and you're just a puppet following a script?"

Dr. Manhattan turns to her, looks Laurie in the eye, and says, "We're all puppets, Laurie. I'm just a puppet who can see the strings."

Like Dr. Manhattan, we too are at the mercy of those things which influence our behavior. The strings of evolution, genetics, nurture, psychology, and group dynamics are having a ball with us. Simply knowing that they exist is not enough to resist their effects. However, knowing that our feelings, thoughts, and behaviors are often influenced by a myriad of invisible reasons can help us come to peace with who we are and our own environmental constants. And hopefully, it will help us be more patient with others as their behavior challenges us.

Chapter 16

Making Sense of it All

When we consider all of the factors that go into makes us who we are, it really isn't so surprising that once in a while we can be less-than-predictable. Human behavior is a confusing chaotic thing, and is an environmental constant that affects us all. And like any other environmental constant, one that gives us ample material with which to create false conditions.

When people upset or frustrate us it's because they are behaving in a manner that we consider somehow inappropriate. Whether people at work are sabotaging our projects, talking behind our backs, taking credit for our work, or failing to deliver on time, we feel wronged. Not just because it's unpleasant but because this sort of behavior is inconsistent with what we consider to be acceptable and predictable. We try to understand it, but sometimes we just can't. And really that shouldn't be very surprising. If the last few chapters have taught us anything it's that human behavior can be, at times, incomprehensible.

Think of it as an algebraic expression, like $12=5+x$. In this case solving for x is pretty straight-forward. Subtract 5 from 12 and you have 7. Put it all together and we get $12=5+7$. Simple, clean, logical—everything we humans long for. The problem is that human behavior is not so predictable, constant, logical, or rational. Trying to figure out human behavior is more like trying to solve for x when $x \approx y\zeta(a \pm \Psi) + \mathcal{X}^f$. There's just no way to approach this expression. What does ζ mean? How can it be plus or minus Ψ? And what's up with that $\mathcal{X}$ icon anyway? As a mathematical problem the expression is meaningless and not deserving of any further scrutiny. But humans are not mathematical expressions; we're people that want to think that we operate in rational and predictable ways. So rather than simply walk away from this problem as utterly absurd, we try to solve for x—human behavior—the best we can. We do this by making assumptions about the variables. So we gather information. We might learn that y is a whole number and a single digit, so now we can narrow that variable down to something between 0 and 9. We might then learn that odds are y is an even number. This leaves us with 2, 4, 6, or 8. Since 6 is kind of in the middle we might select this number as the best option. And so we do this with all the variables of human behavior. We make assumptions based on things like age, gender, religion, ethnicity, and a myriad of other variables. We practice empathy, walking a mile in their moccasins to try and see things from their perspective. All this we do in an effort to understand why someone would behave as they do. Still, try as we might, when it comes to human behavior we can never solve for x. Not even close. The variables are just too numerous and vast. Most of us have a hard enough time solving for our own x—our own behavior—let alone the x of others.

This need to find order and predictability extends far beyond our desire to understand human behavior. It drives the way we approach the world in just about every imaginable way.

Let me show you.

Chapter 17

Order in the Court!

When President Ronald Reagan and Mikhail Gorbachev met in Washington D.C. in December of 1987 the stakes were high. A year earlier in Reykjavik, Iceland, these two sides failed to reach an agreement on the Strategic Defense Initiative, otherwise known as SDI. This meant that the two sides were still entrenched in the very dangerous policy of Mutually Assured Destruction. But this time things were different. Unlike the previous year, the USSR was in an economic free fall. Nuclear arms races are expensive propositions, and Gorbachev could no longer afford to keep up such furious spending. As a result the Soviet leader relented and signed the Intermediate Nuclear Forces treaty, the first agreement to reduce nuclear weapons and a major inflection point in the ending of the cold war.

These facts are in the history books, but what many may not know is that the timing of this summit was no accident. Indeed, summit details such as the location, attendees, menu, agenda, and timing are never left to chance. But in the case of this particular summit great care was taken to build the entire event around one specific moment in time: December 8 at 2 p.m. (EST). The reason for this was simple: This was the time that Nancy Reagan's astrologer told her that Reagan's and Gorbachev's astrological charts best aligned.

As much as we might find Nancy Reagan's

decision to consult an astrologer to help set the President's schedule amusing (or perhaps even a little disquieting), the truth is that she was simply displaying a trait that is common in all of us: A need to find order and meaning in a chaotic universe. Early in our history our need for order gave birth to a variety of superstitions which attempted to rationally explain the world and its invisible forces. Some of these playfully persist today, such as knocking on wood or hanging horseshoes over doorways.

Over time people began to come up with a more complex ways of explaining the workings of these invisible forces that liked to play tiddlywinks with our lives. Divination, such as astronomy, numerology, and other arts came into vogue. Magi looked up to the heavens seeking omens that would help guide everything from important state decisions to when best to plant and harvest the crops. Ancient priests assigned numbers to letters in an effort to find hidden meanings in the scriptures. Prospectors used magical artifacts such as dowsing rods and seer stones to find water, oil, gems, or other treasures. Like superstitions, many of these practices are still widely used around the world today. Case in point, the much beloved Farmer's Almanac bases its predictions for the upcoming year in part on such sources as astronomical signs, planetary positions, and sun spot activity.

Eventually our models for explaining the unexplainable became more and more sophisticated. Religion offered mythologies, histories, allegories, and parables to help us understand the nature of our being and our role in a mysterious universe. Intellectuals, eager to understand the universe through dispassionate and methodical observations, approached the same mysteries through the scientific method. Regardless of the means, be it superstition, divination, mysticism, religion, or science, all serve the same purpose: To offer a construct by which we can superimpose meaning and order over that which seems to have none. Granted, some models are more sophisticated and perhaps even more accurate that others, but in the end they are all offering the same promise: Order.

Given our intense desire to find order in the universe, it should come as no surprise that we attempt to find the same order in our dealings with people. Has anyone ever asked you your sign? Doing so is a way we try to understand someone's behavior based on astrological principles. Tools such as the Myers-Briggs profiles, IQ tests, the DISC assessment, and other psychometric instruments are designed to impose order over human behavior. But understanding human behavior through astrology or even psychological instruments is like trying to measure the width of an atom with a ruler. Still, we try. And what's more, it doesn't matter if the explanations we contrive are correct or not, just so long as they assure us that there's order in the universe and allow us to move on with our lives.

Chapter 18

It's All Good

Sometimes the worth of an explanation offered by one of these models is not determined by its credibility but by the nature of the challenges we're facing at the moment. For instance, medical science may have the most correct and credible explanations regarding the nature of death, but its language of biology and cellular decay won't do much to assuage a grieving mother. For her, at that moment, religion may offer the best answers to help her deal with the pain and grief. Likewise, religion's expertise in prayer, divine intervention, and miracles may help a father as he cares for a sick child, but he's still likely to still seek the services of a physician to help address the child's physical ailments.

With this in mind it should come as no surprise that just as we can see meaning in many constructs, be they superstition, mysticism, religion, or science, we can also find meaning in just about any outcome. We don't tell ourselves that our lives have meaning only if a specific event takes place, or that if something else happens then our existence is devoid of purpose. Our psyches understand that coming to the second conclusion is not beneficial to our well-being, so instead our minds will work hard to find purpose in the outcome, even if it means creating our own meaning.

This ability to find meaning in any outcome can

be seen in a hymn popular in the Church of Jesus Christ of Latter-Day Saints, also known as the Mormon Church, entitled *Come, Come, Ye Saints.* At the time it was written the song's lyrics were meant to embolden the hearts of the Mormon pioneers as they made the treacherous crossing over the plains to the Utah valley. These brave souls endured some of the worst trials in the history of the settlement of the West, yet over and over the hymn repeats the refrain *"All is well! All is well!"* First the hymn declares,

"Though hard to you this journey may appear, All is well! All is well!"

It goes on to say,

"Why should we mourn or think our lot is hard? 'Tis not so; all is right. All is well! All is well!"

And it just keeps getting better!

"We'll find the place which God for us prepared, far away, in the West, where none shall come to hurt or make afraid; All is well! All is well!"

But then the lyrics take a funky turn.

"And should we die before our journey's through, happy day! All is well!"

Wait! What? Die and it's copacetic? Well sure! Then you get to go to heaven, which by most accounts has to be at least as nice as Utah, so why complain?

The song demonstrates how we can find order, meaning, and purpose in any outcome, whether it be arriving safely at our destination with all of our friends and family intact, or dying of fatigue, disease, and starvation along the way.

Chapter 19

The Meaning of Life

One day an organizational director brought her senior staff together for a three-day conference. To break the ice she asked the dozen or so people in attendance this question: If you didn't have to earn a living, what would you do with your time? Many said that they would work for a charitable cause or dedicate their time to some philanthropic effort. One said she wanted to write a book about what it was like to be adopted and meeting her birthmother. Another wanted to write a self-help book for parents struggling to raise handicapped children. After a while a theme began to emerge: People wanted to spend their time doing something which they felt had meaning and could make a difference.

It may be interesting to note that no one said that they would be a senior manager in a high-tech corporation—exactly what they all were.

Like all of us, these staff members wanted to feel a sense of purpose and meaning in what they did. They needed to feel like what they did mattered—and that consequently *they* mattered. Even though these folks were at the height of their careers and were all well compensated, this did not make up for the lack of purpose that many of them seemed to feel in their current positions.

So the question for us is whether we can we find purpose and fulfillment in our current predicaments? After all, we need to earn a living.

Thankfully, the answer is yes. And the way we do this is by robbing the gods of their power.

Chapter 20

Fish Have Fins

Odds are it has been a long time since you've really thought deeply about plankton. After all, what's there to think about? Tiny animals floating passively on the currents, they exist for one reason and one reason only: To be eaten. It's the food source of the entire ocean, the first link in a massive food chain. These little guys are so dedicated to their purpose that they don't even swim, not in the traditional sense anyway. They drift through the oceans on the currents, completely at the mercies of the cosmos.

By and large everything in the ocean, including most fish, has much the same purpose: To be food for some bigger fish. The funny thing is that even thought this is why they exist, most fish don't seem to want to be eaten. In fact, they try to avoid it whenever possible. Danger comes along and they swim off just as fast as they can. What's more, they can. Unlike plankton, fish have muscles and fins that help them escape the ocean's gaping mouths.

If their purpose is to be eaten then no one bothered to tell them.

Like fish, we have fins. We can decide our purpose, even if our chosen purpose is contrary to our true purpose, whatever that may be.

We'll let Charlie Brown show us the way.

In the 1972 animated Peanuts film *Snoopy, Come Home*, Charlie Brown and Linus are milling along the beach when Charlie Brown reaches down and picks up a small stone. Tossing it a couple times in his hand to test its weight, Charlie Brown turns to the ocean and hurls the stone as hard as he can out to sea.

"Nice going, Charlie Brown," says Linus. "It took that rock 4,000 years to get to shore, and now you've thrown it back."

Charlie Brown looks away, exasperated. "Everything I do makes me feel guilty."

Poor Charlie Brown. But as is often the case, this Peanuts cartoon is more reflective of our real-world circumstance than may meet the eye. In this little tale Linus represents the world's tendency to apply meaning to everything, whether it has meaning or not. Philosophy, religion, science, superstition—there's no shortage of constructs eager to offer their interpretation of the meaning of an event. And just like our friend Linus, the interpretation is often more critical rather than it is nurturing.

But like the rest of us, Charlie Brown doesn't need not be at the mercy of such interpretations. Our hero has three options. He can point out to Linus that the rock has no consciousness and therefore no aspirations at all, let alone to one day escape a watery prison. But this is to deny that there's meaning in the universe, and humans crave meaning. Another option may be to accept Linus' assessment of the event and his role in thwarting the rock's 4,000 year journey, but that would leave Charlie Brown feeling bad about himself. Who wants to do that? So what's Charlie Brown to do? Simple. Redefine the meaning of his actions.

"You've got it all wrong," Charlie Brown should have said. "For the last 4,000 years that rock has enjoyed the safety and comfort of the sea. But here on the beach it was dry, alone, and frightened. I simply sent it home."

The hubris! Can he do this? Of course he can. And so can we!

Let's come back to our friend Sisyphus. If his desire is to roll the stone to the top of the hill then he will be forever miserable. This is because his desire is dependent on a false condition—that in order for him to feel a sense of purpose he has to roll the stone to the top, which runs counter to the environmental constant which says the stone cannot be rolled to the top. If he is ever going to be at peace with his endless and meaningless task then something has to change.

The only chance Sisyphus has at peace and fulfillment is to change his objective. By doing this he takes the power away from the gods and takes it for himself. No longer do the gods decide his misery based on the presumed objective of rolling the stone up the hill. Now Sisyphus takes control of his own purpose by taking the objective away from the gods and owning it himself. What might this look like? Maybe he decides that this time he's going to see if he can take a total of 1,000 steps on his way up the hill before the rock rolls back down. Then he'll see if he can do it in exactly 999, and so forth. Then later he might see if once the rock starts rolling down he can beat it to the bottom. After that he might compose a song on the way up, then just for kicks, sing it backwards on the way back down.

It really doesn't matter what objectives or purpose he sets for himself, just so long as they are his own. That way success is always a possibility, and where there's the possibility of success there's purpose. Sure, the gods may say that success looks like the rock making it all the way up the hill, but that's impossible and therefore should be discarded as an objective. Rather than banging his head against a wall (or in his case a stone) for all eternity, trying to force success where success is impossible, Sisyphus needs to instead decide what success looks like for himself and go after that. He's still doing what the gods commanded, but not for the purpose they commanded. As a result he has robbed them of their punishment, and consequently their power.

This is what it means to live in harmony with environmental constants; to do that which has been assigned us but for our own purposes.

This is what Viktor Frankl did during WWII when he was imprisoned in a Nazi concentration camp. In his book, Man's Search for Meaning, Frankl talks about the absolute need mankind has for meaning, explaining that purpose must be found in every moment and in every action we take, especially when others seek to rob us of our meaning and replace it with their own torturous purposes. Just as in the gods had imposed an impossible purpose on Sisyphus as an eternal punishment, the Nazis tried to strip away all vestiges of humanity from Frankl, and with that, his purpose and meaning. If we use Frankl's experience as an example, the false condition that would have been torturous to him was the feeling that he should be treated with the respect and dignity that should be afforded to any man. Is this unreasonable? Of course not! But it was not likely to be forthcoming from his captors. This left Frankl with three choices: Allow his captors to decide his worth and wither away and die from despair, fight the guards and attempt to escape, likely resulting in his death, or live in harmony with his environmental constants and do all that was asked of him, but for his own purposes. He chose the last, and in so doing may have saved his own life as well as many of those around him.

All of these people—fictional or otherwise—learned how to live in harmony with their environmental constants, and in so doing found a sense of meaning and purpose in their work. The task before us is learning to do the same.

Chapter 21

Learning to Live in Harmony

Living in harmony with environmental constants is not the same as giving into them, or even fighting them. When we fight something we're attempting to defeat it, but as we know, environmental constants cannot be defeated. Giving into them would mean accepting the meaning and purpose offered by the world. Living in harmony, on the other hand, means coping with our environmental constants, but for our own reasons.

Consider the way the whale makes its home in the sea. The water is no less wet for the whale than it is for the fish. Nor does the whale try to fight wet water. However, these creatures clearly live by their own rules in this environment. Wet water says there's no air down here, so the whale had better grow some gills real fast. The whale says "Nah, that's cool. We'll just go to the surface to breathe."

"Okay," says wet water, "but it's cold in here and we leach heat away something fierce. Best you just become cold-blooded like the rest of the fish."

"No, that's okay. But thanks," the whale says. "We'll just grow a lot of blubber. We'll be fine."

No doubt water is starting to get a little miffed at this point. "But there's nothing big enough down here to feed such mammoth warm-blooded creatures such as yourselves."

"We'll eat krill and plankton."

"Krill and plankton?! Are you nuts? You're the biggest mammals that have ever existed on this planet and you're going to eat some of the tiniest creatures living in the sea?"

"Yeah. It'll be cool," the whale says almost as an afterthought. He's so disconnected from water's conditions that he doesn't see why this conversation is so bewildering to the liquid.

"Wait, wait," wet water says, now completely exasperated. "This just won't work. You give live birth. I mean, you nurse your young on milk, for crying out loud! And hello! You have no lips!"

"That's okay. We'll manage. We're not asking you to change your nature."

If we think about our friend Sisyphus we see that he lives in harmony with his environmental constants, not because he fights his plight or gives into it, but because he continues to fulfill all of the requirements of his sentence but for his own reasons.

In addition to the whales, Month Python can also teach us something about living according to our own purposes in a frustrating and meaningless world. In perhaps the most famous of Python films, Monty Python and the Holy Grail, the hero King Arthur sets forth on a quest to find the Holy Grail. In the course of his travels he runs across the most absurd assortment of circumstances imaginable. This befuddles Arthur. To him, seeing order and meaning in the absurdity is vital. One group he encounters though has learned how to live in harmony with the absurdity.

In one scene Arthur comes across a couple of peasants toiling in the mud. He calls out to one of them, presuming her to be an old woman, only to learn that he's actually a 37-year old man named Dennis. Arthur apologizes for the misunderstanding but Dennis isn't satisfied.

"What I object to is you automatically treat me like an inferior," Dennis says.

"Well I am king..." This is Arthur's attempt to restore order to a situation which, by his reckoning, has become completely absurd and unacceptable. After all, who ever heard of a peasant talking back to a king? The idea is so inconceivable that the only conclusion Arthur can come up with is that the guy simply doesn't know who he is.

"King of the who?" asks Dennis' companion. King Arthur tells her that he is king of the Britons, and that we're all Britons, and that therefore he was their king. Again; bringing reason to chaos.

"I didn't know we had a king," the woman says. "I thought we were an autonomous collective."

Whether toiling as serfs under the fist of a merciless lord, or working to the will of an autonomous collective, the nature of their work doesn't change. What changes is the reason they are doing the work. This is what it means to live in harmony with environment constants. Dennis and the woman are not rebelling directly against Arthur, Briton, or the monarchy system of government. They are not organizing an underground conspiracy bent on toppling Arthur from his throne. What they are doing is rejecting the idea that they should view themselves as inferior peasants and serfs, nothing more than disposable humanity, good only for enriching their feudal lords for no more reward than for the privilege to live on the land and eat remnants. Of course this doesn't change what is required of them. They are still toiling in the filth, collecting sod or whatever it is that they were doing in the muck, but they're not doing it because the lord has decreed it (though of course he has); they're doing it for their own reasons.

So what is our purpose? If not for money and recognition, why do we do what we do? Let's see if we can't figure this out.

Chapter 22

We Don't Matter—Sort Of

One day I was sitting next to a river and noticed a small ant making its way across a rock along the river's edge. Then a wave of water swelled up and washed the ant away. Maybe it drowned right away, maybe not. Either way, without the support of the rest of the colony that ant was dead.

So what changed in my world?

Nothing, as far as I could tell.

Every moment of every day trillions of organisms are dying all over the world, yet everything continues, just as it has the last ten thousand years and likely will for the next ten thousand.

But this book isn't concerned with ants or other tiny organisms. We're talking about people, and people matter much more than ants, right? After all, some of our closest friends are people. We need to believe that what we do is important and that we matter. Of course we do matter, and the contributions we make in the workplace are important. However, it's easy to lose perspective of what really matters.

Imagine a series of concentric circles radiating out from the center, like a target or a bullseye. (Actually you don't need to imagine it; it's right below.) In the center of this bullseye is ourselves, followed by our families on the next ring, then our friends. The next ring would be our co-workers, followed by our organization, finally by our company. I call it the What Really Matters Bullseye.

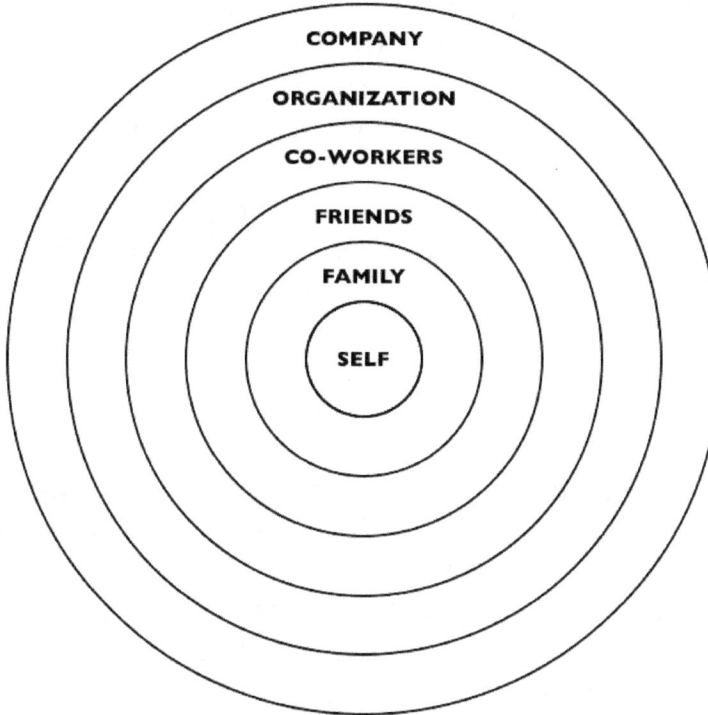

WHAT REALLY MATTERS BULLSEYE

Now think about this: Right now, at this very moment, a man in India named Amit just died. Okay, maybe not. Maybe it was Alberto in Costa Rico, Manfred in Germany, or Fyodor in Russia. The point is that someone somewhere just died. So, here's the question: How have we been affected? Odds are not at all. There are over 6.7 billion people on this planet and the majority of these folks have absolutely no bearing on our lives, and in return we have no impact on theirs. Or to put it another way, to most people, we don't matter. You could die right now and the vast majority of humanity wouldn't blink an eye.

So before we start getting too depressing and toss this book in the trash bin, let's bring it in closer —much closer. Let's go back to the bullseye and start at the center—Self. Now ask yourself this question: If you were to die right now, would this person be effected. Well yeah! It's you! Clearly our day-to-day lives would be seriously thrown out of whack if we were to die. Okay, so we matter to ourselves. Good to know.

Now let's go out to the next sphere—our families. Without a doubt they would be significantly impacted if we were to pass away. Children would miss their parents, spouses would miss their companions, and parents would miss their children. Entire lives could be changed forever, even reaching into future generates. The emotional and psychological toll that a loss in the family can have cannot be over-stated. Then there are the financial considerations. While mercenary in comparison to the emotional trauma, the loss of a provider can have profound consequences from which families may never recover. The verdict? Yes, we matter to our families.

Next are our friends. Relationships between friends can be very strong, almost as strong as family. The feeling of loss would be great among those close to us, but the same level of dependence likely doesn't exist. A child only has one father, but a friend has other friends, not to mention other sources of emotional and financial support. Still, our presence would be sorely missed.

Now let's look at the workplace. What would happen there if we were to suddenly disappear? Well the answer here is more nuanced. Our coworkers would most certainly miss us, though not all for the same reasons. Those with whom we have close personal relationships would miss us for quite some time, but that would fall more in the Friend circle. Those that needed to suddenly pick up our workload would miss us until a replacement could be found, but make no mistake, a replacement would be found. Life would eventually return to normal for these people. Our customers would have to learn to work with different people, but that's not a significant trial for them, nor would it be any of the other professional relationships we have. Eventually we'd be replaced and all would go back to the way things were. So yes, we do matter to our coworkers—kinda.

What about the organization we work for? In the same way that those that have to do our work would be impacted by our absence, the organization we work for would be affected as well, but just barely. Others would pick up wherever we left off, so the work would still get done. Eventually they would have to recruit, hire, and train a replacement, but that sort of thing happens every day. A few projects might have to be pushed out to the next quarter or maybe even cancelled altogether, but the organization would persist. Our absence would certainly not cause HR, Marketing, Finance, Manufacturing, or any other group to fold. So do we matter? Well, a little it can be supposed. Hiring and training folks is a hassle and can be expensive, so we matter in as much as our presence avoids all of that rigmarole.

That brings us to the last sphere as far as the company is concerned—the company itself. In a corporation of any real size our disappearance would scarcely be noticed. Employees come and go every day, and as much as we like to think we're different, few of us are. In short, we don't matter. Don't believe me? Quit and see how long it takes for the company to go out of business. It would probably take about as long as it did when the last guy quit. He thought he mattered, too.

Yeah, it sucks, but that's the ugly truth of it. But don't worry. Bear with me a little bit longer. Things will pick up.

Chapter 23

Golden Handcuffs

The tragic irony is that while we don't matter much to our jobs, our jobs matter a great deal to us. As we've already learned, we often allow our jobs to establish our sense of self-worth to those that most depend on us, particularly our families. Our families rely on us for support, and that support comes by way of our employment. All of this means that our companies define us much more than we define the company. To put it in another way, we need our jobs more than our jobs need us.

As you can imagine, there's real danger in allowing your job or company to have such a hold on your sense of self-worth and value. This isn't healthy and needs to change. Just as Sisyphus had to rob the gods of their power to take control of his own purpose, we too need to deny our jobs the power to determine our own worth. After all, we're more than just employees. It's important that we derive meaning from the multiple facets of who we are. True, we're employees, but we're also students, parents, children, siblings, spouses, and neighbors. We're members of religious, political, social, and other organizations. We're also emotional, spiritual, physical, and intellectual beings with purpose. We express ourselves through the arts, athletics, hobbies, and exploration. In short, we're complicated creatures that derive our meaning through all sorts of roles we play, and no one of them should own defining who we are, least of all "employee".

Chapter 24

Figuring Out What Matters

Okay, so how do we do this?

The first step is to decide what give us meaning, purpose, and a sense of fulfillment in our lives. For example, let's say that after careful reflection you decide that nothing is more important than family. Nothing matters if you fail as a spouse and as a parent.

The second step is to decide what constitutes success in this purpose. If we've decided that family is first and foremost in our lives then we need to figure out what a successful family looks like. Maybe it's children doing well in school and spending time doing healthy activities. We may decide that a close and caring relationship with our spouse is a requisite for a successful family. There are other things as well. Physical safety at home, the opportunity to spend time as a family, chances for the children to learn and grow. The list could go on, but you get the idea. You need to decide what's most important for yourself.

Third, we need to identify what actions and behaviors support these new priorities. For example, if we've decided that giving our children plenty of opportunities to learn, grow, and experience life is vital to a successful family then we need to decide what actions would help make that happen. Maybe it's providing music lessons or opportunities to play after-school sports. This would mean that we need to be available in the evenings, be there to help them practice, encourage them to do well, and earn the money necessary to pay for these sorts of opportunities.

Red flag! Notice that one of the actions is to earn the money needed to pay for lessons and the like. This puts us right back at work. Once again our jobs are defining our purpose. Right? Wrong. Remember that our friends Sisyphus and Dennis did not stop doing what they needed to do; they continued to do these things but for their own purposes. Likewise, we're still working, but not out of loyalty to the company, bigger offices, new fancy titles, or recognition from our leaders and peers. We're now working to help us raise our families.

So what has this new mindset done for us? Well, let's test it. Let's say that during your performance review you receive a 3% raise when you were expecting a 5% raise. How do you respond? Well, if like my good friend you measure your worth by the size of your house or the numbers on your paycheck then you have just been told that you're worth 2% less than you'd thought. But you're not her. You're you; someone that defines yourself as a family member. So what's changed? Nothing. And everything. The difference between 3% and 5% will have no bearing on what you need to provide for your family, so the number is meaningless. So you smile, thank your manager for his or her time, and walk out the door and get back to work. Nothing has changed; you're still a person of significant worth and value with a clear and noble purpose.

Congratulations. You just robbed the gods of

their power.
    Okay. Now how do we do this?

Chapter 25

What Makes You Tic?

Everyone finds meaning and purpose in different aspects of their lives. Some, like the person in our example, find purpose in raising their families. Others find meaning in providing services, while others still gain a sense of fulfillment though perfecting themselves physically, intellectually, or spiritually. There are as many reasons for being as there are people—certainly more than any assessment, no matter how well designed, could ever measure.

But hey, what's a book like this without a cheesy personality test, right?

The Cheesy Self Purpose And Meaning assessment, or as I call it, the Cheesy SPAM test, is designed to help identify those aspects of our lives that give us the greatest meaning and sense of fulfillment.

Instructions

Below is a list of 60 activities many people enjoy. Rate the degree to which you find these activities personally fulfilling and rewarding on the following scale:

2 - This activity is rewarding to you most of the time

1 - This activity is rewarding to you some of the time

0 - This activity is not very rewarding to you

Rate these activities:
1. _____ Attending worship services
2. _____ Reading non-fiction
3. _____ Trying different kinds of food
4. _____ Participating in sporting activities
5. _____ Meeting new people
6. _____ Spending time with your spouse or partner
7. _____ Spending time with your children or parents
8. _____ Earning / saving money
9. _____ Helping others improve themselves
10. _____ Attending community or sporting events
11. _____ Participating in politics
12. _____ Using public transit
13. _____ Reading spiritual material
14. _____ Watching documentaries
15. _____ Going to an art gallery, museum, or a play
16. _____ Exercising daily
17. _____ Experiencing different cultures
18. _____ Hearing about your spouse's or partner's day
19. _____ Hearing about your children's day
20. _____ Raising your standard of living
21. _____ Explaining ideas to others
22. _____ Attending parties, rallies, or other events
23. _____ Doing charitable work
24. _____ Recycling and reusing
25. _____ Praying or meditating

26. _____ Learning new things
27. _____ Listening to different kinds of music
28. _____ Eating right / healthy
29. _____ Trying something new for the first time
30. _____ Helping with your partner's projects
31. _____ Helping with your children's projects
32. _____ Having good health and life insurance
33. _____ Instructing others
34. _____ Taking with your neighbors
35. _____ Donating to charity
36. _____ Using less energy
37. _____ Contemplating spiritual matters
38. _____ Contemplating ideas deeply
39. _____ Painting, singing, or playing an instrument
40. _____ Being strong and healthy
41. _____ Traveling to new places
42. _____ Doing activities with your spouse or partner
43. _____ Doing activities with your children
44. _____ Being able to afford family wants
45. _____ Helping others feel good about themselves
46. _____ Working with others
47. _____ Caring for the less fortunate
48. _____ Hiking, fishing, or camping
49. _____ Telling others about your faith

50. _____ Considering scientific problems
51. _____ Reading fiction
52. _____ Testing your physical strength or endurance
53. _____ Saying you've done something unique
54. _____ Talking with your spouse or partner
55. _____ Talking with your children
56. _____ Seeing to your family's safety
57. _____ Helping others see new opportunities
58. _____ Spending time with friends
59. _____ Volunteering to help others
60. _____ Conserving resources

Scoring the results

Now it's time see how we scored. Add up the scores associated with each aspect. Each will have five scores that will add up to a number between 0 and 10.

Coach

Add up the scores for questions 9, 21, 33, 45, 57

___ + ___ + ___ + ___ + ___ = Coach score

Cultural

Add up the scores for questions 3, 15, 27, 39, 51

___ + ___ + ___ + ___ + ___ = Cultural score

Discovery

Add up the scores for questions 5, 17, 29, 41, 53

___ + ___ + ___ + ___ + ___ = Discovery score

Environmental
Add up the scores for questions 12, 24, 36, 48, 60

___ + ___ + ___ + ___ + ___ = Environmental score

Intellectual
Add up the scores for questions 2, 14, 26, 38, 50

___ + ___ + ___ + ___ + ___ = Intellectual core

Parent
Add up the scores for questions 7, 19, 31, 43, 55

___ + ___ + ___ + ___ + ___ = Parent score

Partner
Add up the scores for questions 6, 18, 30, 42, 54

___ + ___ + ___ + ___ + ___ = Partner score

Physical
Add up the scores for questions 4, 16, 28, 40, 52

___ + ___ + ___ + ___ + ___ = Physical score

Security
Add up the scores for questions 8, 20, 32, 44, 56

___ + ___ + ___ + ___ + ___ = Security score

Service
Add up the scores for questions 11, 23, 35, 47, 59

___ + ___ + ___ + ___ + ___ = Service score

Social
Add up the scores for questions 10, 22, 34, 46, 58

___ + ___ + ___ + ___ + ___ = Social score

Spiritual
Add up the scores for questions 1, 13, 25, 37, 49

___ + ___ + ___ + ___ + ___ = Spiritual score

Now turn to the Aspects Radial and color in each attribute according to the combined score for that attribute. For example, someone with the scores listed below will color in the Aspects Radial accordingly:

Coach: 1 + 1 + 1 + 2 + 1 = Combined score: 6

Cultural: 2 + 1 + 2 + 0 + 0 = Combined score: 5

Discovery: 1 + 2 + 2 + 2 + 2 = Combined score: 9

Environmental: 1 + 2 + 2 + 2 +

1_ = Combined score: _8

Intellectual: 2_ + _2_ + _2_ + _2_ +
1_ = Combined score: _9

Parent: 1_ + _1_ + _1_ + _1
+ _1_ = Combined score: _5

Partner: 2_ + _2_ + _2_ + _2_ +
2_ = Combined score: _10

Physical: 1_ + _1_ + _2_ + _2_ +
2_ = Combined score: _8

Security: 1_ + _1_ + _1_ + _2_ +
1_ = Combined score: _6

Service: 0_ + _2_ + _2_ + _1_ +
2_ = Combined score: _7

Social: 0_ + _0_ + _1_ + _1_ +
0_ = Combined score: _2

Spiritual: 1_ + _2_ + _2_ + _2_ +
1_ = Combined score: _8

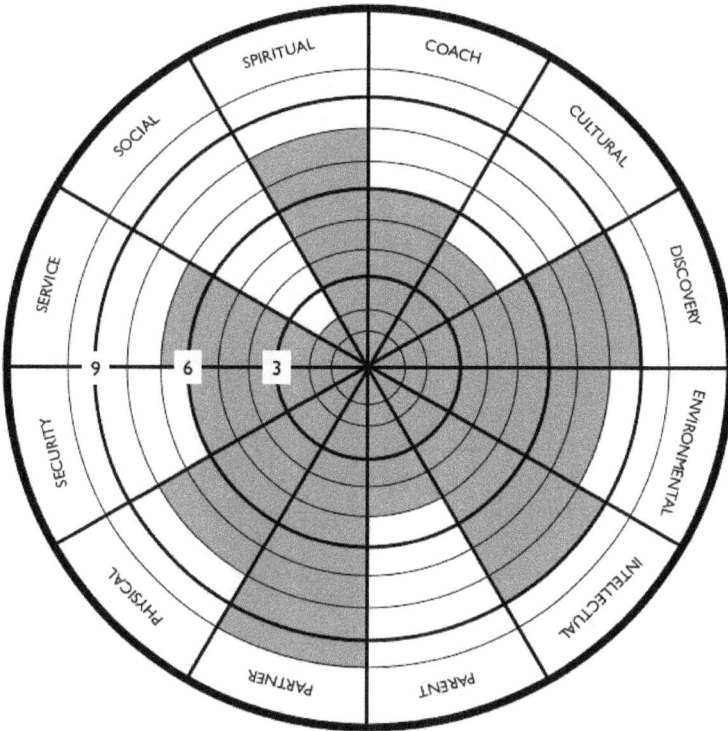

SAMPLE ASPECTS RADIAL

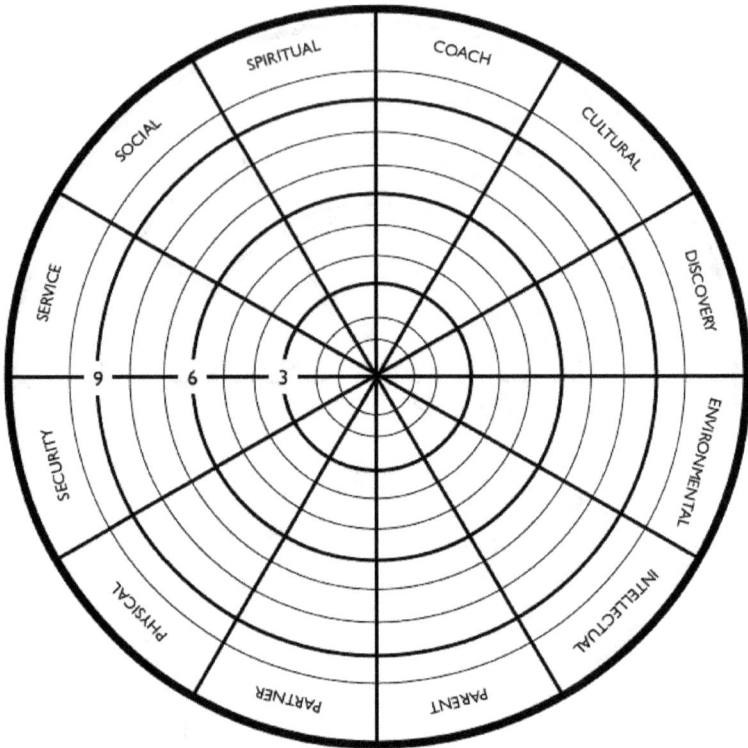

ASPECTS RADIAL

Okay. Now that you have completed the Cheesy SPAM test, let's see if we can't figure out what floats your boat. Remember, the goal here is not to change what you do; it's to change why you do what you do. We want to do what we do for our own reasons, for our own purposes. So how do we do this? Let's see how some of these character aspects can help guide our motivations.

Chapter 26

Coach

If you scored high in Coach then you're the sort of person that finds fulfillment in helping others learn and grow. It gives you a deep sense of satisfaction when you help others develop as individuals, whether it be personally, professionally, academically, athletically, or in any number of ways that people better themselves. You understand the important and pivotal role that a mentor and coach can play in helping people develop to their full potential. You watch with satisfaction as people develop their skills and open up new opportunities for themselves. It gives you purpose, knowing that the skills you have worked so hard to develop will live on through the next generation.

What do I do with this?

Since you gain a sense of fulfillment from helping others develop, this is where you can find satisfaction in your job. Demonstrate your expertise in all that you do, not for the sake of the company, but for the sake of others that may be watching and emulating you. You may have some formal mentor and training relationships, but think of all that you do as an opportunity to help others see and understand how to perform with quality, and then perform with quality. Understand that your legacy isn't tied to the company but rather to the continued progress of your profession in others.

Chapter 27

Cultural

As someone that scored high in Cultural, you derive a great deal of enjoyment from the creative arts. Maybe you're an amateur or budding musician, or perhaps an artist, or someone who enjoys singing in a local choir. It could be that you're one of those people that "gets" independent cinema, or still enjoys attending plays. You may even be someone that has attended opening night of a new art gallery. Regardless of your outlet, culture plays a major role in defining your purpose in life. You marvel at how creativity, technique, and hard work can come together to create something so sublime, so seemingly effortless. Culture takes you places, causes you to re-examine your own life, and makes you wonder what is possible. It can leave you feeling enriched and blessed, and at the same time empty and confused.

What do I do with this?

At work you may not produce paintings, music, literature, or sculptures, but you do produce art—of a sort. You can find purpose and fulfillment in your work by producing in a way that you find aesthetically pleasing, creative, thoughtful, or compelling. Expressing yourself through your job is key. For you, robbing the gods means doing your very best for the sake of you art, not for the sake of the company.

Chapter 28

Discovery

If you scored high in Discovery then you find meaning in experiencing the world. You're eager to try new things, travel to new places, eat new foods, try anything that's new and exciting. Adrenaline junkies that jump out of airplanes one day, go scuba diving the next, and then drive their motorcycles across the desert the third are Discovery types. But this doesn't mean that all Discovery types are psychotic, hair-on-fire daredevils. Even small experiences can give you a sense of joy and wonder. The excitement lies not in the size of the experience but rather its newness, as well as what you discover about yourself and others in the process. You see the world as a cornucopia of experiences to be had, all calling to you from every direction.

What do I do with this?

The world is your oyster, and work is no different. Sure, your job has its repetitive aspects, but as the saying goes, you can never step in the same river twice. Every day is a new day, and with it the promise of new experiences. This can be especially true at work where change and chaos can seem par for the course. Instead of resisting change, embrace it as a chance to experience something new. Each day you go to work and do your best, just to see what new experiences the day may have in store for you.

Chapter 29

Environmental

Those that scored high in Environment feel a sense of purpose in caring for the planet. You understand that there's a connection between you and the environment, and that to care for yourself and others means to care for the environment. It's clear to you that much of what we enjoy today is thanks to limited resources that we're quickly depleting, and that our well-being, as well as that of future generations, depends on how wisely we use and conserve these resources. You're ever taken in by the natural beauty of this world and want to keep it safe and unspoiled.

What do I do with this?

You may find new ways of conserving resources in the course of your job. Every moment at work you're using office supplies, power, water, even the energy you consumed in the way of food. Finding ways to do your job just as well—perhaps even better—while using fewer resources can give you a great deal of satisfaction. What's more, as others see what you do they, too, may follow your example, thereby magnifying your contributions all the more.

Chapter 30

Intellectual

If you scored high in Intellectual then you're one of those people that feel a sense of fulfillment in exercising your intellect and considering matters introspectively. People such as yourself like to think things out, to mentally explore the world and consider new ideas. Reading, studying, and observing may be some of your favorite activates. You enjoy seeing the big picture, connecting the dots, and synthesizing new understandings. You find that from time to time you enjoy being alone to think and consider what you've learned or observed. You're also fairly introspective, always examining yourself and how you relate to the world on an intellectual level. You're the sort of person who enjoys taking classes and learning new things, no matter the subject.

What do I do with this?

Your sense of purpose and fulfillment at work may be increased by approaching your job in a more intellectual fashion. Consider the work you do as an ongoing experiment in which there's no right or wrong responses to stimuli—just responses to be observed, measured, and considered. You may even develop hypotheses as to how things will proceed and see what you can learn from the outcome of these field experiments.

Chapter 31

Parent

Those of you that scored high in Parent find fulfillment through your relationship with your children. Parenthood can be a strong motivator. As the saying goes, children are the future, and raising up that future is an important responsibility, one that can provide a strong sense of purpose and fulfillment to a parent. You understand that being a parent means more than simply providing your offspring with food, shelter, clothing, and a public education. It means raising them up to be moral, happy, and productive members of society. To accomplish this you need to provide a loving, nurturing, and secure environment where children can thrive. It also means providing avenues for them to grow, experience the world, and discover who they are, whether that's through sports, music, theater, travel, art, or any number of other extracurricular activities. You also feel a real responsibility to play a major role in your children's education, whether that means helping them with homework, developing a relationship with the school and faculty, guiding them as they struggle to learn social skills, or even homeschooling.

What do I do with this?

If you work to provide all you can for your children then the frustrations or even the triumphs you encounter at work pale in comparison to those you experience at home. You understand that your legacy rests with your children and future grandchildren, not with the contributions you make at work. Your best strategy may be to keep the What Really Matters Bullseye first and foremost in your mind and let the issues you experience at work take a backseat as you focus on what's really important to you—your children. This means doing the very best you can at work for them, not the company.

Chapter 32

Partner

If you scored high in Partner then you find fulfillment through your relationship with your spouse or partner. You're one of those lucky people that's partnered with your best friend. You recognize that a partner can be a friend, a support, a coach, a therapist, and a lover all rolled into one. They're there to celebrate with us when we feel wonderful, and console us when we feel down. They encourage us when we're nervous, and give us a reality check when we're feeling cocky. They accept us for who we are, but want us to become better. They think we're the very best thing that has ever happened to them, when we know darned well that it's the other way around.

What do I do with this?

The trick to using your relationship with your partner as the center of your purpose at work may lie in learning to become the person you think your partner deserves. Work will always present challenges. When this happens, your response to these challenges should be based on what sort of person you want to be for your partner, not for the company. You will perform brilliantly; not for the company, but for your partner.

Chapter 33

Physical

People that scored high in Physical experience a sense of purpose and reward through exercising their physical selves. You feel a great deal of satisfaction and accomplishment as you reach physical goals, win a race, or beat a personal record. You love the high you get as the endorphins begin to flow, your blood pumps, your muscles tingle, and your competitive juices excite the senses. The idea of being the very best, the fastest, the strongest, or the most skilled motivates you. It may be that the technical aspects of your sport excite you intellectually as well. Measuring progress, even in the hundredths of a second, can provide all the motivation you need to redouble your efforts.

What do I do with this?

One way you might consider using the sense of purpose you derive from physical activity is by scheduling your day around workouts and training. Let's say that you have a long list of things that need to be done throughout the day. Scheduling and sequencing these tasks in such a way that you can take an extra half hour at lunch to train can be the purpose you assign to your job. That way you're not doing your job effectively and efficiently for the company, you're doing so for yourself and your training schedule.

Chapter 34

Security

Those of you that scored high in Security feel a sense of purpose in their ability to provide security for themselves and others. Security is one of our most fundamental needs. Without it we cannot easily reach past our immediate circumstances. Scoring high in Security means that you find meaning and purpose in your ability to give yourself and others the security they need to feel safe to chase after those more self-actualizing goals in life. You're mindful of your retirement and may even have specific goals concerning when and how much you hope to have saved by then. You're not a big risk-taker, choosing instead to take the proven path to success, even though it may take longer and be more difficult. Consistency is the name of the game for you.

What do I do with this?

As you work hard for the company, do so for the sake of securing a future for yourself and those close to you. This means getting additional training and developing new skill sets, not to be of value to the company for the company, but to be of value to the company for you and your loved ones.

Chapter 35

Service

If you scored high in Service then you're someone that finds purpose and fulfillment in your own life by improving the lives of others. Helping others is a strong motivator for you. The idea of turning something bad into something good exhilarates you. You have a highly developed sense of empathy that helps you understand the pain and suffering that others. You believe that life has been particularly good to you and feel a need to give something back. There's also the thought that by helping others you yourself grow, develop, and in general become a better person. Discovering that you can do something that you thought was beyond you is particularly satisfying. You also have a generally positive outlook for the future of humanity and feel that making the world a better place tomorrow begins with taking a single step today. In all, it makes you feel good to know that you're able to help people that, for whatever reason, are unable to help themselves. Their joy becomes your joy.

What do I do with this?

Since helping and serving others gives you a great deal of satisfaction, you should look for ways to line up the nature of your work with the goodness of service. One idea might be to look inside the organization at those around you. Your coworkers may not be starving and homeless, but everyone has needs that they cannot meet on their own. Another way might be to look at how the products or services your company delivers help those in need. As one company's motto puts it, it's not what you make; it's what you make possible. The products and services that your company delivers can be the seeds for some extraordinary causes and acts of service. Sure, the degrees of separation night be pretty deep, but that doesn't matter. You're still a contributor.

Chapter 36

Social

People that score high in Social experience fulfillment through their relationships with others. It gives you joy. Human beings are social creatures, and you're the creature-ist of us all. You value your close friends and in turn are a good friend to them. You frequently talk with strangers as though you've known them for years. For you, spending time with others is time well spent. You enjoy the closeness, the camaraderie, the feeling that comes with knowing that there are people that you care about in the world and that care about you. Furthermore, you enjoy supporting and serving your friends whenever possible.

What do I do with this?

There are few places where social bonds can come in handy as much as in the work environment. Think of what you do as a way of developing and strengthening your social relationships. This means that you do what you do, not for the good of the company, but for the good of those in your social circle.

Chapter 37

Spiritual

People that score high in Spiritual find purpose and meaning in the spiritual aspects of their lives. You're someone that feels a deep connection with that higher power, the great architect of the universe. You know that there's more beyond the physical world around you, something greater that holds promise for the future, either in this life or in the life to come. This gives you a feeling that you're being watched over and cared for, as well as a sense of love and acceptance from the universe, no matter the circumstance. You belief that there's more to this world than that which the sum total of your five senses can describe. You have faith in things which you cannot see, touch, or hear, but which you know are there nonetheless. This faith gives you a sense of right and wrong in your life, and a feeling of love and compassion for those around you. This moral compass often directs how you engage with people and the world around you. It motivates you to live a better life and to help those that stand in need to do the same.

What do I do with this?

Dedication to a higher law can be a powerful source of purpose and fulfillment, even in the workplace. Connecting your work to those things which your faith espouses might be a good place to start. Let's say that your faith values patience, kindness, caring, and longsuffering. What better place than a chaotic work environment to perfect these character traits? When challenges, disappointments, and conflicts arise, approach them with the purpose of perfecting yourself and helping others do the same.

Chapter 38

It Takes Practice

Learning to let go of our old mindsets and live according to our own purposes is no easy task. It doesn't just happen overnight. It takes time, practice, self-examination, reflection, failure, recommitment, and patience. Think of it as an athlete working to increase her flexibility. She doesn't just wake up one morning and say "I'm going to do the splits". She has to work at it each day, stressing her muscles and tendons, increasing her range imperceptibly day by day for months, maybe even years, before she can do the splits. The process is slow, painful, and difficult to measure, but those that are patient and persistent will eventually see results.

Chapter 39

Then Again, I Could Be Wrong

Toss a frog into a pot of boiling water and he'll hop out just as fast as he can. Hot water is not an environmental constant for this little guy, and furthermore he's not powerless to change it, so hop away he does. But drop the frog in a pot of cool water and slowly turn up the heat and that little critter will float about happily in the water until he boils to death. Why? Well, barring any cool technology that would enable us to talk to a dead frog, we can't say for sure. But remember, we love meaning and order, so let's see if we can't make up our own answer.

Maybe in the beginning, when the water was cool and pleasant, he decided that this was nice and so there was no need to do anything. This changed over time, of course, but the changes were so small, gradual, and imperceptible that he may not have noticed them. Then, before too long, his environment was killing him. Problem is that by this time he'd probably forgotten what the cool pleasant water felt like, figured that this is what it had been like from the beginning, and that he would be just fine. So in the end we have a frog in the boiling water, completely and utterly miserable, on the verge of death, telling himself that there's nothing he can do about it. He's telling himself that boiling water is an environmental constant and that wishing it to be anything but is a false condition.

It's a good thing that frog legs are delicious.

The frog's story leaves us with word of caution: Not all unpleasant states are environmental constants that cannot be changed. Some states can and must be changed. No doubt some of the new world colonists living under the tyrannical rule of the British in the 1700s thought that things like taxation without representation and indiscriminate search and seizures were simply realities of their station. To these citizens the idea of fighting the crown must have seemed completely futile. Regarding this situation as wet water would have been tragic indeed for the U.S.

The task before us is to wisely discern environmental constants from immensely difficult challenges that require a great deal of blood, sweat, and tears, but which, nonetheless, must be changed. This is a common dilemma for all of us, one expressed is a short poem called the Serenity Prayer, which in part reads as follows:

God grant me the serenity
to accept the things I cannot change;
courage to change the things I can;
and wisdom to know the difference.

The poem was made most famous by Alcoholics Anonymous who used the verse to help its members keep perspective along their journey to sobriety. No doubt many suffering from alcoholism felt that quitting the hooch was an impossibility and that they could never be happy without a drink now and again. These people incorrectly assumed that, for them, alcoholism was an environmental constant, when in fact it wasn't. Furthermore, they clung on to the false condition that told them that without alcohol they couldn't be happy. Clearly, hanging on to such ideas is very dangerous.

Of course alcoholics don't have a monopoly on clinging to the idea that something cannot be changed when it can. Those suffering from obesity, poor physical fitness, drug addictions, and other unhealthy lifestyles often tell themselves that there's nothing they can do and so why try.

There's another poem, less celebrated than the Serenity Prayer, though the author is known to many around the world. Mother Goose wrote:

For every ailment under the sun
There is a remedy, or there is none;
If there be one, try to find it;
If there be none, never mind it.

Both poems teach the same idea, that we shouldn't worry ourselves over things we cannot control, but that we need to find the courage and wisdom to change that which we must.

Okay, but where do we start?

Chapter 40

Worry About Your Own Pond

There's a saying that tells us to think globally and act locally. The idea is to recognize that there are global challenges that we must face, but that the best way for us to tackle these problems is to work locally to try to solve these issues. Worried about human rights in Tibet? The rainforests in Brazil? Good. You should be. But really, what can you do that would have a significant impact? Write a check? Buy a necklace from the region? Write as letter? Hold up a sign outside the governor's mansion? Here's another idea: Work to improve the lives of those in your community. All you have to do is look and it's easy to see that there are people all around us that are suffering. The elderly, the mentally and physically disabled, those lacking adequate healthcare. Our communities are full of people in need and that could use our help. And how about the environment in your neighborhood? The environment is all part of one gigantic open system. Improving it where you live improves it for the entire planet, so why not work to save it where you have the most impact? Okay, so it's not as sexy or glamorous as Tibet or Brazil, but it matters all the same. And what's more, you have much more direct control over what's happening in your own community than you do in some far-off land. Furthermore, if everyone around the world were to focus on making things better where they lived then, lo and behold, global problems would essentially vanish. It's like the old saying, count the pennies and the dollars take care of themselves. The world is nothing more than a network of local communities, so fix the communities and you fix the world.

Remember the What Really Matters Bullseye? We can have the most impact on the world by focusing on those closest to us.

Chapter 41

Now Go Forth and Thrive!

So there you go, the secret to finding purpose, meaning, fulfillment, and ultimately greater peace and happiness while working with idiots on the most pointless tasks ever conceived by man. And thank goodness, too. We all have to earn a living and—more importantly—feel a sense of value and self-worth. In the past we've wondered if it's possible to do both, but now we know we can. We're pretty incredible creatures, we humans. We can do some amazing things, if we apply ourselves and find meaning in our work. So however you do it, figure out what turns your crank and go after it. You don't need to quit your job or completely change careers (though don't rule out those possibilities). All you need to do is discover what matters most to you and how you can do that in your job. After all, you're the center of your own bullseye.

About the Author

Lon Schiffbauer, Ph.D. is an organizational culture expert who believes that when employees are engaged in what the company is trying to accomplish on a personal and meaningful level, great things can happen. Lon has over 25 years experience working and consulting with such companies as FedEx, Intel, eBay, and other global companies that differentiate themselves based on culture. In addition to his consulting work, Lon is a faculty member at the University of Phoenix where he teaches a variety of undergrad and graduate-level business strategy courses. He holds a Bachelor's degree in Journalism, an MBA, and a Ph.D. in Industrial/Organizational Psychology. For his dissertation Lon studied the effects of the pursuit of self-esteem on an employee's ability to thrive in the workplace.

www.ingramcontent.com/pod-product-compliance
Lightning Source LLC
Chambersburg PA
CBHW070544030426
42337CB00016B/2338